THE GUARDS

The Guards and the mounted regiments of the Household Cavalry are the guardians of the monarch and stand proud in their duty everyday across London. They form the Household Division and are the most celebrated of soldiers with a global reputation for 'ceremonial perfection'. The division comprises seven regiments, headed by the Life Guards and the Blues and Royals who form the Household Cavalry Regiment (HCR). immaculate in their polished silver cuirasses and helmets. They can be identified by the red tunics worn by the Life Guards and the blue worn by the Blues and Royals.

The Foot Guards stand in order of seniority, with the Grenadiers first followed by the Coldstream, Scots, Irish and Welsh Guards. This structure of precedence is illustrated by the manner in which each regiment within the Foot Guards wears the buttons on its ceremonial uniform. The Grenadiers wear theirs in ones, the Coldstream in sets of two, the Scots in threes, the Irish in sets of four and the Welsh in fives.

All seven regiments have a prime responsibility at state ceremonial occasions, including the King's Birthday Parade, known as Trooping the Colour, the State Opening of Parliament, state visits, the annual national Act of Remembrance at the Cenotaph and numerous bespoke events of national importance. While tourists see the public duty role of the Household Division, the men and women of these regiments are also trained to operate across the spectrum of combat operations. The HCR delivers armoured reconnaissance, while the Foot Guards are infantry soldiers trained to operate in all environments from the jungle to desert warfare, as well as supporting a Guards parachute platoon. Since their formation, all have deployed on operations in both World Wars, most of the post-war conflicts and more recently in Iraq and Afghanistan. The ability to mount these dual capabilities is often referred to by soldiers as the 'red and green skills' and the division prides itself on being highly trained and ready for all operations.

The courage of the divisions' soldiers was highlighted in 2012 when LCpl James Ashworth of the Grenadier Guards was decorated with the highest award possible for his valour in Afghanistan. After being dropped by helicopter in Helmand Province, he and his colleagues came under heavy fire. Ashworth led his team in a charge over 300 metres to the heart of the enemy position in a nearby village where two insurgents were killed in the initial assault. In the subsequent fighting the young LCpl used his last grenade to eliminate a Taliban sniper who threatened his team but was himself shot down. His citation stated: 'LCpl Ashworth made the ultimate sacrifice and showed extraordinary courage to close on a determined enemy.' He was awarded the Victoria Cross.

David Reynolds Editor

The Grenadier Guards prepare for ceremonial duty at the Major General London District, summer dress inspection. (MOD/Crown Copyright)

CONTENTS

CONTENTS

3 **Welcome**
The Guards and the two mounted regiments of the Household Cavalry stand proud in their duty every day across London. In parade they deliver precision, splendour, discipline, and excellence.

6 **The Household Division**
The troopers of the Life Guards and the Blues and Royals that make up the Household Cavalry, along with the Guardsmen of the five regiments of Foot Guards, form the seven regiments of the Household Division, serving their King and country as guardians of the monarch. They are unique in their ceremonial and combat capability.

22 **The Household Cavalry**
The Household Cavalry contains the British Army's most high-profile regiments, often deployed across the globe on operations. It consists of the Life Guards and the Blues and Royals, with a sabre squadron from each serving with the mounted regiment on public duties in London.

38 **The Grenadier Guards**
The Grenadier Guards is the senior regiment of the Foot Guards. Famous throughout the British Army for its flawless ceremonial drill and combat readiness, the Grenadiers has most recently been deployed in the Middle East.

56 **The Coldstream Guards**
The Coldstream Guards is the oldest continuously serving regular regiment in the British Army. Although founded earlier than the Grenadiers, the regiment was placed second to them in the order of precedence, as the Grenadiers had spent longer in the service of the Crown.

72 **The Scots Guards**
The Scots Guards is Scotland's regiment of Foot Guards. From the Battle of Waterloo to the rocky slopes of Mount Tumbledown in the Falklands, then into Iraq and Afghanistan, the Regiment has served the monarch for five centuries.

88 **The Irish Guards**

Members of the Irish Guards are universally known as 'The Micks'. They dress the buttons on their tunics in sets of four to signify their position in the Foot Guards. In addition to its ceremonial excellence, the main role of the 1st Battalion Irish Guards is to deliver dismounted infantry.

102 **The Welsh Guards**

The Welsh Guards is the Welsh nation's finest, representing the principality on ceremonial duties where its soldiers can instantly be recognised by the buttons on their red tunics, dressed in two sets of five to highlight that the Welsh Guards stands as the fifth regiment of Foot Guards.

ISBN: 978 1 80282 743 9
Editor: David Reynolds
Senior editor, specials: Roger Mortimer
Email: roger.mortimer@keypublishing.com
Cover design: Dan Jarman
Design: SJmagic DESIGN SERVICES, India
Advertising Sales Manager: Brodie Baxter
Email: brodie.baxter@keypublishing.com
Tel: 01780 755131
Advertising Production: Debi McGowan
Email: debi.mcgowan@keypublishing.com

SUBSCRIPTION/MAIL ORDER
Key Publishing Ltd, PO Box 300, Stamford, Lincs, PE9 1NA
Tel: 01780 480404
Subscriptions email: subs@keypublishing.com
Mail Order email: orders@keypublishing.com
Website: www.keypublishing.com/shop

PUBLISHING
Group CEO: Adrian Cox
Publisher, Books and Bookazines: Jonathan Jackson
Published by
Key Publishing Ltd, PO Box 100, Stamford, Lincs, PE9 1XQ
Tel: 01780 755131
Website: www.keypublishing.com

PRINTING
Precision Colour Printing Ltd, Haldane, Halesfield 1, Telford, Shropshire. TF7 4QQ

DISTRIBUTION
Seymour Distribution Ltd, 2 Poultry Avenue, London, EC1A 9PU
Enquiries Line: 02074 294000.

We are unable to guarantee the bonafides of any of our advertisers. Readers are strongly recommended to take their own precautions before parting with any information or item of value, including, but not limited to money, manuscripts, photographs, or personal information in response to any advertisements within this publication.

© Key Publishing Ltd 2023
All rights reserved. No part of this magazine may be reproduced or transmitted in any form by any means, electronic or mechanical, including photocopying, recording or by any information storage and retrieval system, without prior permission in writing from the copyright owner. Multiple copying of the contents of the magazine without prior written approval is not permitted.

THE HOUSEHOLD DIVISION

THE HOUSEHOLD DIVISION
GUARDIANS OF THE MONARCH

The Life Guards and the Blues and Royals form the Household Cavalry Regiment serving alongside the five regiments of Foot Guards within the Household Division. (MOD/Crown Copyright)

6 THE GUARDS

'Septem Juncta In Uno'
Seven Joined In One

The mounted troopers of the Household Cavalry and the guardsmen of the five regiments of Foot Guards form the seven regiments of **the Household Division**, serving their King and country as guardians of the monarch. From ceremonial duty in London to combat operations across the world, the men and women of this unique formation are truly ready for anything.

With a worldwide reputation for 'ceremonial perfection', the Household Division (HD) also has an equally impressive combat pedigree. Since the early 20th century all seven of its regiments have been deployed on operations in different areas of the world, including taking part in both World Wars. During the post-World War Two era, they were deployed to a number of overseas theatres including Malaya, Borneo, Cyprus, the Suez Canal Zone, Aden, Northern Ireland, the Falkland Islands and, more recently, Iraq and Afghanistan.

In September 2022, members of The Queen's Company of the 1st Battalion Grenadier Guards bore the coffin of Her Majesty Queen Elizabeth II at her state funeral; within days, they were packing away their bearskins and tunics before deploying to the Middle East on operations.

The Household Division's seven regiments comprise the Life Guards and the Blues and Royals, which form the Household Cavalry Regiment (HCR) and the Household Cavalry Mounted Regiment (HCMR), as well as the five regiments of Foot Guards: the Grenadier, Coldstream, Scots, Irish and Welsh Guards. The troops of all seven regiments are highly trained in the full spectrum of their respective operational roles, ranging from armoured reconnaissance to jungle and desert warfare, as well as providing the members of the Guards Parachute Platoon that forms part of B Company of the 3rd Battalion the Parachute Regiment.

Every year millions of tourists visiting London watch the Household Cavalry and the Foot Guards conducting their ceremonial roles known as 'public duties'. The mounted soldiers of the HCMR can be seen at Horse Guards in Whitehall, immaculate in their polished silver cuirasses and helmets. Meanwhile, the Foot Guards, resplendent in their iconic scarlet tunics and bearskins, parade daily at the Tower of London, Buckingham Palace, St James's Palace, and Windsor Castle.

While manning these posts can be demanding, the number of them is greatly reduced from the sentry duties listed in September 1818. In those far-off days members of the Foot Guards stood proudly at a total of 89 different locations across London. In addition, there were three-night guards provided at the Bank of England, Drury Lane Theatre and Covent Garden Opera House, as well as the guard provided at the Tower of London. The global ceremonial brand of the Household Division is so strong that these regiments have their own 'celebrity status' with images of both the Foot Guards and Household Cavalry adorning merchandise in tourist shops across the capital; while at Heathrow Airport travellers can buy a 6ft tall child's teddy bear – dressed as a Guardsman.

The Ranking of the Regiments

The Household Division is headed by the Household Cavalry. The Life Guards is the most senior, though not the oldest, regiment of the British Army. It evolved from a royal bodyguard raised in the 1600s, at the end of the English Civil War, when a number of Royalists followed Prince Charles, later King Charles II, into exile. This body was always on duty, escorting and shielding him from danger, and by the time of the Restoration of the

THE HOUSEHOLD DIVISION

The Grenadier Guards, the senior of the five regiments of Foot Guards which includes the Coldstream, Scots, Irish and Welsh Guards. (MOD/Crown Copyright)

The Foot Guards and the Household Cavalry Mounted Regiment mount daily guards across London. (DPL)

monarchy in 1660, it had swelled in number to more than 500 and was organised in three units: the King's Troop, the Duke of York's Troop, and the Duke of Albemarle's Troop. At that stage it was known as the Horse Guards or Life Guard of Horse. In 1788, a troop of Horse Guards and Horse Grenadier Guards were incorporated into what was by then the Regiment of Life Guards.

Their comrades in today's Blues and Royals can trace their history back to the Regiment of Horse raised by Cromwell in 1650. After he returned from exile to Britain, King Charles II incorporated these mounted troops in part of his own Army, naming them the Royal Regiment of Horse. The colour blue had long been associated with them and it remained when they became part of the new army commanded by Aubrey de Vere, the Earl of Oxford, whose livery was blue. The regiment later became the Royal Horse Guards and were dubbed The Blues. In 1969, the Royal Horse

The Household Division is headed by the Household Cavalry. The Life Guards is the most senior, though not the oldest, regiment of the British Army. (MOD/Crown Copyright)

8   THE GUARDS

The Foot Guards and the two Household Cavalry regiments have established responsibilities at state ceremonial occasions, including the King's Birthday Parade, also known as Trooping the Colour. (MOD/Crown Copyright)

The Garrison Sergeant Major, the most senior Warrant Officer in the Foot Guards, is responsible for the delivery of ceremonial excellence at all events. (MOD/Crown Copyright)

Trooping the Colour, the State Opening of Parliament, state visits, the annual national Act of Remembrance at the Cenotaph and numerous other events of national importance. In addition, every day throughout the year the Household Cavalry and the Foot Guards mount public duties across London.

Three Original Foot Guards

Until 1900, the Brigade of Guards was made up of just three regiments, the Grenadier, Coldstream, and Scots Guards. The Irish Guards was added to the Brigade on April 1, 1900 at the wish of Queen Victoria, to commemorate the courage of the Irish regiments who served in the Boer Wars. In 1915, a fifth regiment was raised after widespread support for Wales to be represented in the Foot Guards. The Secretary of the War Office announced on February 11, 1915 that a regiment would be created. He said: "The King has been graciously pleased to sanction an addition to the Brigade of

Guards were amalgamated with the 1st or Royal Dragoons, better known as the Royals, with the formal title of the Blues and Royals (Royal Horse Guards & 1st Dragoons).

Within the Household Division the Foot Guards form the Guards Division which, until 1968, was called the Brigade of Guards. The five regiments stand in an order of seniority, with the Grenadiers first, followed by the Coldstream, Scots, Irish and Welsh Guards. This structure of precedence is illustrated by the manner in which each regiment wears the buttons on its ceremonial scarlet uniform. The Grenadiers wear theirs in ones, the Coldstream in sets of two, the Scots in threes, the Irish in two groups of four and the Welsh in two of five. The Foot Guards and the two Household Cavalry regiments have prime roles at state ceremonial occasions, including the King's Birthday Parade, also known as

The Irish Guards was added to the Brigade in April 1900 at the wish of Queen Victoria to commemorate the courage of the Irish regiments in the Boer Wars. (MOD/Crown Copyright)

THE GUARDS 9

THE HOUSEHOLD DIVISION

The Foot Guards and the two Household Cavalry regiments have traditional roles at ceremonial occasions, many of which have a historical legacy. (MOD/Crown Copyright)

THE HOUSEHOLD DIVISION

The Coldstream Guards parades its Regimental Colour at House Guards Parade. It was initially formed as The Lord General's Regiment of Foot Guards. (MOD/Crown Copyright)

Regiment is made a regiment of grenadiers in commemoration of their having defeated the grenadiers of the French Imperial Guard". As a result, the regiment began wearing the bearskin cap, which hitherto had been a distinction of French grenadier companies.

The origins of the Coldstream Regiment of Foot Guards lie in Cromwell's 'New Model Army'. It was first known as 'Monck's Regiment of Foot', which mustered near Berwick in Northumberland and fought with distinction at the Battle of Dunbar in 1650. General Monck moved his headquarters to Coldstream in Berwickshire in 1659 and it was from there that he and his regiment began its historic march to restore order in London in 1660 in readiness for the exiled King Charles II to be restored to the throne. Charles II had been in the Netherlands and arrived back in London on his birthday. The Coldstream Guards paraded on Tower Hill on Valentine's Day, February 14, 1661 to become The Lord General's Regiment of Foot Guards by the formation of a battalion of Welsh Guards." For a short period up to 1920, there was a sixth regiment of Foot Guards called the Guards Machine Gun Regiment, which provided Number 8 Guard at the King's Birthday Parade in 1919. In December 1950, the Household Cavalry joined with the Brigade of Guards to become the Household Brigade, later re-named the Household Division in July 1968. The Brigade of Guards then became the Guards Division.

The 1st or 'Grenadier' Regiment of Foot Guards was formed in Bruges in 1656 to protect King Charles II during his exile. It was to become the King's Regiment of Foot Guards following the Restoration in 1660. On July 29, 1815, after the regiment's success in the Battle of Waterloo against the French, the *London Gazette* announced that, "the 1st

Guardsmen fighting in World War One faced challenging conditions and often fought wearing their gas hoods, due to the fear of a German mustard gas attack. (MOD/Crown Copyright)

The newly raised 1st Battalion Welsh Guards mounted King's Guard on St David's Day 1915. Many of its soldiers were recruited from other Guards regiments. (MOD/Crown Copyright)

Guardsmen of the 5th Battalion Coldstream Guards enter the town of Arras in France as they head towards Germany in September 1944. (MOD/Crown Copyright)

Guards. Since that day they have proudly served the sovereigns, both at ceremonial events and in most major conflicts.

The Scots Guards can trace its origins back to 1642 when the regiment was raised by Archibald, Marquis of Argyll. Its seniority as the third regiment dates from when it became part of the English establishment. Known as the Scots Fusilier Guards, the regiment served in the Crimean War where its soldiers won five Victoria Crosses for outstanding valour. Among them was Private William Reynolds, 27 years old, whose gallantry at the Battle of the Alma in the Crimean Peninsula later resulted in his being awarded the Victoria Cross. On September 20, 1854, when the regiment's Colour came under attack he rallied his comrades around them.

The VC was introduced on January 29, 1856 by Queen Victoria to reward acts of supreme valour, and was awarded retrospectively to include such acts performed during the Crimean War. Pte Reynolds was the first private soldier in the Scots Fusiliers to receive the award and he later achieved the rank of corporal. Today, his VC is displayed at the Scots Guards Regimental Headquarters in Wellington Barracks, London.

In 1877, Queen Victoria changed the name of the Scots Fusilier Guards to the Scots Guards and in 1899 Her Majesty presented it with a State Colour, which is still carried on parade on special occasions. The regiment's pipers wear kilts of Royal Stuart tartan and blue doublets, originally with glengarry bonnets, but these were replaced by feather ⟶

Guardsmen of the 1st Battalion Welsh Guards in France in World War Two. Battalions from five regiments of the Foot Guards saw extensive service across Europe and Africa during the war. (MOD/Crown Copyright)

THE GUARDS 13

THE HOUSEHOLD DIVISION

All seven regiments of the Household Cavalry and Foot Guards served in Northern Ireland in the 1970s on a deployment named Operation Banner. (DPL)

bonnets with blue and red hackles (the colours of the Household Division) on the orders of King George V in 1928.

At the outbreak of war on August 4, 1914, the 1st Life Guards were stationed at Hyde Park, while the 2nd Life Guards were based at Regent's Park and the Royal Horse Guards at Windsor. In 1916, Life Guards reservists were formed into the Household Battalion, a unit which fought as infantry for the rest of the war until it was disbanded in early 1918. In late 1918, both regiments gave up their horses and reformed as the 1st and 2nd Guards Machine Gun Battalions, reverting to their former identities and roles shortly after the Armistice. In 1922 the two regiments, the 1st and 2nd, were amalgamated to become The Life Guards.

The Arrival of the Welsh

On March 1, 1915, the Welsh Guards mounted its first King's Guard on St David's Day, just weeks after its formation in February, at which the soldiers wore wartime khaki uniforms. The new regiment was soon in France and Belgium amidst the horrors of trench warfare. On one occasion the guardsmen returned from the front line for a rest period and found their newly formed regimental band waiting to meet them. The musicians led them for the last couple of miles back to their base at the village of Méaulte, in northern France, playing their regimental march, *The Rising of the Lark*, for the first time.

With the exception of the Welsh Guards, the Foot Guards fought at the first battle of Ypres in late 1914 and across the Western Front. Life in the trenches was very hard, the troops enduring poor food and, more often than not, living in deep mud with the constant threat of shelling by artillery and the fear of a gas attack. At Passchendaele in August 1917, the Guards took part in an advance of two and a half miles, a major achievement in such terrible conditions. As a young officer, Winston Churchill, Britain's later wartime Prime Minister, trained with the Grenadier Guards for a month to learn about trench warfare.

During World War Two, the Life Guards and the Royal Horse Guards were reformed into two units: the 1st Household Cavalry Regiment and 2nd Household Cavalry Regiment. The former, mainly consisting officers and men of the Life Guards, saw service in Palestine, Iraq, Syria, Persia, North Africa and Italy, and at the end of the war took part in the advance into Germany. In 1944, the 2nd Household Cavalry Regiment (HCR), predominantly comprising members of the Royal Horse Guards, was assigned to the Guards Armoured Division as an armoured reconnaissance regiment for the invasion of Normandy and the subsequent advance north through France and Belgium. Thereafter it led the way north through Holland towards Nijmegen and Arnhem during Operation Market Garden.

In 1945, following the end of the war in Germany, the 1st and 2nd HCR were reformed as the Life Guards and Royal Horse Guards, both equipped with armoured cars. At the same time, each provided a mounted squadron

The Scimitar's armoured reconnaissance vehicle of the Household Cavalry has supported units of the Foot Guards and the wider Army on exercises and operations across the globe. (DPL)

14 THE GUARDS

The Foot Guards and the Household Cavalry regularly take part in 'out of area' exercises to maintain their infantry skills. (DPL)

THE HOUSEHOLD DIVISION

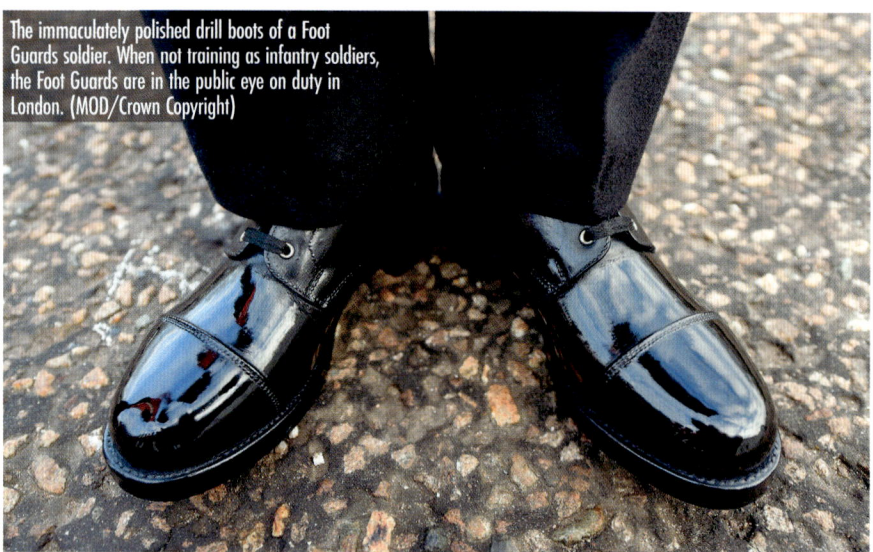

The immaculately polished drill boots of a Foot Guards soldier. When not training as infantry soldiers, the Foot Guards are in the public eye on duty in London. (MOD/Crown Copyright)

to form the Household Cavalry Mounted Regiment (HCMR) for ceremonial duties in London.

Before and After World War Two

During the post war years, the Life Guards saw service in Egypt, Aden, Oman, Malaya, Hong Kong, Cyprus, Germany and Northern Ireland, and were deployed for the last time as the Life Guards in the First Gulf War of 1991. Meanwhile, the Royal Horse Guards served in Germany, Windsor, Northern Ireland, and Cyprus. In 1969, the Royal Horse Guards were amalgamated with the Royal Dragoons to become the Blues and Royals (Royal Horse Guards & 1st Dragoons). In 1982, the Blues and Royals provided two troops as an armoured reconnaissance element for the British task force in the Falklands Conflict. Ten years later, in 1992, the Life Guards and Blues and Royals were amalgamated to form the HCR, whilst retaining their individual regimental identities. The role of the HCR was that of the formation reconnaissance regiment for 1st Armoured Infantry Brigade. In 2014, the regiment's role was changed to that of armoured cavalry, conducting reconnaissance and surveillance, both mounted and dismounted.

All five regiments of the Foot Guards saw extensive service throughout World War Two. On the outbreak of war, a British Expeditionary Force (BEF), including a number of Guards units, was deployed to France to defend its borders, but saw little action in the ensuing period dubbed 'The Phoney War'.

In April 1940, a Guards Brigade took part in the ill-fated campaign against the invading German forces in Norway.

Within a short period of time, the BEF was being evacuated from the beaches of France and Belgium, with the Guards battalions putting up a fierce resistance at Boulogne, Arras, and Dunkirk in the face of heavy fire from German armour and air attacks. Meanwhile in North Africa, British forces were facing the German Afrika Korps and Italian forces in Egypt. In Western Europe, Guards formations landed at Normandy in June 1944, after a lengthy period of training. They took part in heavy fighting to capture a key objective, the town of Caen.

Then on September 17, 1944, the Guards Armoured Division led 30th Corps and spearheaded the advance of the British Second Army, the ultimate objective of which was to cross the Rhine and link up with Allied

The Household Cavalry deployed to the Falklands in the 1980s with its Scimitar and Scorpion light armoured vehicles, while both the Scots and Welsh Guards joined 5th Brigade. (DPL)

16 THE GUARDS

A sniper serving with the Household Division operating on the outskirts of Basra city shortly after the 2003 invasion of Iraq. (MOD/Crown Copyright)

The Household Cavalry and the Foot Guards have served in almost every military operation of the past two centuries, with the most recent being Afghanistan. (MOD/Crown Copyright)

airborne forces before advancing on the German industrial heartland of the Ruhr. In the event the advance encountered heavy resistance from German troops. Following the German surrender on May 7, 1945, the Guards Armoured Division conducted mopping up operations and occupation tasks. On June 9, 1945, having been selected for conversion back to infantry, it held a 'farewell to armour' parade on Rotenburg Airfield in Lower Saxony, in Germany.

In December 1950, King George VI decreed that the Household Cavalry should be brought under the command of the Major General Commanding the Brigade of Guards and that the incumbent should in future be known as the Major General Commanding The Household Brigade. In July 1968, it was renamed the Household Division (HD) and has remained as such ever since. The Major General appointed to command the HD was, and remains, a Guards general and simultaneously holds the appointment of General Officer Commanding London District, based in Headquarters Horse Guards in Whitehall.

The post of Garrison Sergeant Major was appointed to military districts from the mid-1800s. It largely involved administrative duties across the formation, such as billeting, furnishing and other duties. In London, the nature of the role began to change with the appointment of Garrison Sergeant Major George Stone in 1952. An Irish Guardsman, he identified what might be called a 'skills-fade' in ceremonial drill across the Foot Guards. This had inevitably happened after the priority of warfare across Europe and beyond. Stone took it upon himself to oversee the drill preparations and training for the State Funeral of King George VI, following which the role of Garrison Sergeant Major became increasingly associated with ceremonial occasions.

The 1970s and Beyond

In 1971, almost two years after the start of 'The Troubles' in Northern Ireland, which saw British troops deployed on the streets of Northern Ireland during the period 1969-1999, the 1st Battalion Grenadier Guards was deployed to Northern Ireland at a week's notice. Stormont, the government in the Six Counties, had requested further military support from Westminster to help restore order after weeks of rioting had left the police exhausted and overwhelmed. This emergency tour for the Grenadiers came just five days after the battalion had finished a tour of public duties. A year later a battalion of Grenadiers was sent from its base at Munster in Germany on a four-month operational tour in Londonderry. During the following 30 years it was a similar story for the Coldstream, Scots, and Welsh Guards, all of which served numerous operational tours in Belfast and the rural areas of County Tyrone, Fermanagh, and South Armagh during the 30 years long internal security campaign in Northern Ireland.

New technology is constantly being introduced, such as drones used as 'eyes in the sky' to locate the enemy and identify threats. (MOD/Crown Copyright)

THE GUARDS 17

THE HOUSEHOLD DIVISION

In 1982, after Argentine forces had invaded the Falklands, both the 2nd Battalion Scots Guards and 1st Battalion Welsh Guards accompanied the rest of 5 Infantry Brigade when it sailed to the South Atlantic to take part in Operation Corporate – the battle to retake the islands. On Mount Tumbledown the Scots Guards fixed bayonets for a night attack assault on Argentinian positions in what became a bloody hand-to-hand battle in pitch darkness. The Scots Guards was successful in storming the mountain and overcoming all resistance, but in doing so lost eight men killed and 43 wounded. The Welsh Guards, meanwhile, had faced what proved to be the worst single loss of life in the Falklands Conflict when the landing ship on which the regiment was embarked, the Royal Fleet Auxiliary *Sir Galahad*, was bombed by Argentine A4 Skyhawk fighter-bombers while waiting to disembark at Bluff Cove. A total of 48 men died and 94 were injured.

Nine years later in 1991, following Saddam Hussein's decision to send his forces into Kuwait, the Guards were yet again in action. The Grenadiers, Scots and Coldstream Guards deployed to Kuwait as part of Operation Granby in what later became known as the First Gulf War. Meanwhile, a potential humanitarian crisis in the Balkans saw regiments and units of the HCR deployed to the region in the early 1990s – initially on a United Nations peacekeeping mission which later transitioned to become the follow-on Stabilisation Force in Bosnia and Herzegovina (SFOR).

The War on Terror

The terrorist attacks on the United States of America in September 2011, in which more than 3,000 people were killed, resulted in a US-led military intervention into Afghanistan, which Britain supported, to help the Northern Alliance eject the Taliban from power. Meanwhile, a Coalition, that included Britain, supported the United States' invasion of Iraq in 2003. Among the initial forces to arrive was D Squadron of

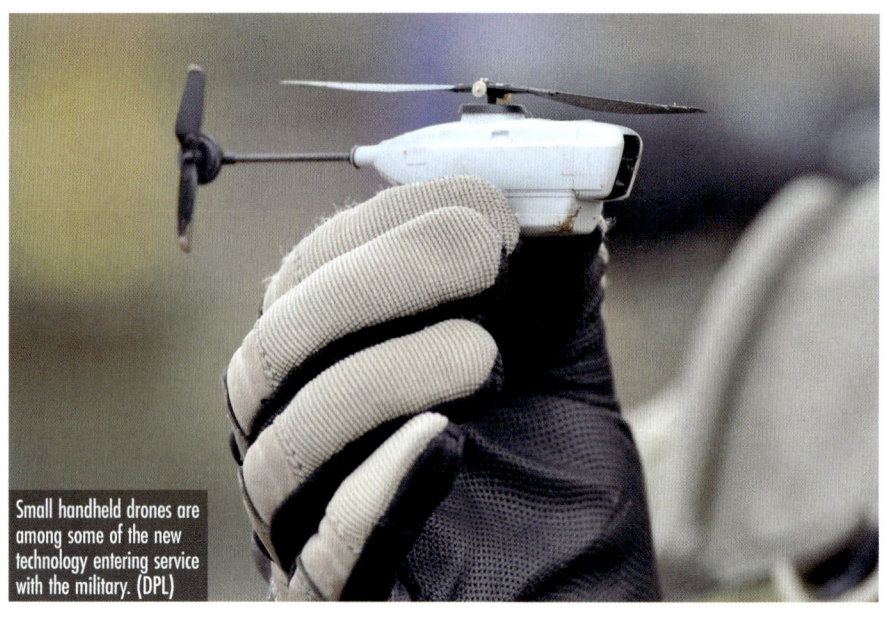

Small handheld drones are among some of the new technology entering service with the military. (DPL)

While the Household Cavalry moved across Helmand in Afghanistan in Scimitars, the Foot Guards relied on Chinook helicopters and armoured vehicles. (DPL)

The Household Division was deployed in Afghanistan where both the Foot Guards and the Household Cavalry served on the frontline. (MOD/Crown Copyright)

Warthog and Viking tracked armoured vehicles were used by the Foot Guards in Afghanistan and, as the conflict progressed, Mastiff, Cougar and other protected vehicles were deployed to Helmand. (DPL)

the HCR, which deployed as the formation reconnaissance squadron for 16 Assault Air Assault Brigade, leading the force into southern Iraq. In a tragic incident, however, the squadron was the victim of a friendly fire incident involving an attack by a USAF A-10 Thunderbolt on their Scimitar CVR-T in which Lance Corporal of Horse Matty Hull was killed. In a separate incident, Lieutenant Alex Tweedie, and Lance Corporal Karl Shearer of the Blues and Royals both died when their Scimitar overturned in an irrigation canal.

The Irish Guards, the Grenadiers, Coldstream, Scots, and Welsh all served in Iraq, with some detached to Baghdad to provide force protection at a small British base inside the Green Zone. In April 2004, B and C Squadrons of the HCR deployed to Iraq, and in June 2007 A and C Squadrons returned.

As the so-called 'war on terror' continued, NATO planned to expand its security and stability mission in Afghanistan, while at the same time delivering reconstruction and development. A number of NATO teams had already been established in Kabul since 2001, with new projects emerging in the north and west. In 2005, the UK government agreed to support an expansion of security into southern Afghanistan, with UK forces moving into Helmand. In 2006, D Squadron, HCR, deployed with 16 Air Assault Brigade on what became a 'break-in battle' to secure control of southern Afghanistan, which had been dominated by insurgents and narco-criminals. The squadron's Scimitar light tracked vehicles provided fire support to troops on the ground and it used its Spartan command vehicles to evacuate injured soldiers. Some of the Blues and Royals personnel were involved in one of the worst incidents of the tour when their vehicle was ambushed. Second Lieutenant Ralph Johnson of the Blues and Royals, Captain Alex Eida of the Royal Artillery and LCpl Ross Nicholls of the Royal Signals were killed, and several others seriously injured. In a second incident, LCpl Sean Tansey died in an accident while repairing a Scimitar.

The Foot Guards operate machine guns mounted in Land Rovers using WMIKs (Weapons Mounted Installation Kits). (DPL)

A Welsh Guards patrol waits for orders to advance towards a village compound in Afghanistan. (DPL)

THE GUARDS 19

THE HOUSEHOLD DIVISION

Chinook helicopters provide the element of speed and surprise – allowing troops to fly into an area to conduct a search for weapons and depart quickly. (DPL)

passing of Her Majesty Queen Elizabeth II. The procession, which was directed by Garrison Sergeant Major WO1 Vern Stokes of the Coldstream Guards, was headed by dismounted detachments of the Life Guards and the Blues and Royals who formed up on the forecourt of Buckingham Palace each side of the centre arch, with the Life Guards on the north side and the Blues and Royals on the south side.

As the funeral procession moved off a guard of honour from the 1st Battalion Coldstream Guards stood on the paved area outside the forecourt in Queen's Gardens, facing west. It comprised three officers and 101 soldiers. The escort and bearer party from The Queen's Company, 1st Battalion Grenadier Guards, was positioned in The Quadrangle, while Scots, Irish and Welsh Guards lined the streets. As the coffin and procession arrived at the Palace of Westminster, the Grenadiers of The Queen's Company carried the coffin from the gun carriage and placed it on a raised platform, known as a catafalque, in Westminster Hall. The HD later escorted Her Majesty to her final resting place at Windsor. ●

The Foot Guards deployed on successive tours to Helmand with the Grenadiers, Coldstream, Scots, Irish and Welsh sometimes collaborating with each other. In the spring of 2009, the Welsh Guards deployed as part of 19 Light Brigade and took part in Operation Panther's Claw – a major mission to clear insurgents from the town of Lashkar Gah. It was to be a harrowing period for the Welsh Guards in particular, which lost three officers, one of them its commanding officer, Lieutenant Colonel Rupert Thorneloe.

Then in October 2009 the Grenadier Guards arrived as part of 11 Light Brigade. Just a month later, on November 3, a rogue Afghan policemen shot dead five soldiers, among whom were three Grenadiers Guards and two members of the Royal Military Police attached to the battalion. All five had been mentoring with the Afghan police in a compound where they had been living and eating together.

In September 2022, the HCR and all five regiments of the Foot Guards took centre stage in the military ceremony to mark the

One of the Life Guards pauses in red ceremonial uniform alongside his fellow troopers in green combat clothing, during an exercise in the Egyptian desert to remember those who died at El Alamein. (DPL)

As the operation in Afghanistan came to an end in 2014 and regiments handed bases and responsibility over to the Afghan National Army, vehicles were cleaned and flown back to the UK. (DPL)

The Household Division spearheads the ceremonial escort at Her Majesty Queen Elizabeth II's state funeral, with the Grenadier Guards providing the bearer party. (MOD/Crown Copyright)

1st and 2nd Battalions entered Brussels. Then on September 20, tanks of the 2nd Battalion and troops of the 1st Battalion crossed the Nijmegen Bridge. In 1945 the Guards' tanks were part of the first British unit to cross the Siegfried Line on the German border and in March the Guards units quickly advanced deep into Germany, despite many of their Churchill tanks needing maintenance. After the war Grenadiers stood down from their armoured role and reverted to infantry.

In the post-war years, the regiment served across the globe from Palestine, to Cyprus, Borneo, Malaya, British Guiana, and an internal security deployment to Belize.

The Troubles

Sectarian conflict in Northern Ireland exploded in 1969 and the Grenadiers was one of the first regiments to see operations in Ulster. Throughout the 30-year campaign, known as Operation Banner, the regiment served in Londonderry, Belfast, and South Armagh – the

The town of Crossmaglen in South Armagh where three Grenadiers died in 1974. (DPL)

latter being dubbed 'bandit country' by the media. In 1977 a Grenadier Guards officer, Captain Robert Nairac GC, was on his fourth tour in the Province, working as a liaison officer for 3rd Infantry Brigade. On the night of May 14, 1977, he was abducted and murdered by the Provisional IRA.

In late 1978 the Grenadiers were sent to South Armagh, their headquarters located at Bessbrook with companies based at Crossmaglen, Newtownhamilton, Forkhill and Newry. Number 2 Company was based in Crossmaglen, a town known as XMG and located at the RUC station just off the main square in the Cullaville Road. The main town of Crossmaglen was small and when patrols left the base they were watched by spotters for the Provisional IRA (PIRA). On December 21, 1978, Sergeant Garmory was in charge of a patrol of 12 men on patrol. The Guardsmen were in three four-man patrols, one at each end of the town and one responsible for the centre. Sgt Garmory's patrol, call sign 24 Lima, was in Newry Road and he was the lead man with the light machine gun deployed to his rear and two Guardsmen across the street. As per their training, the Guardsmen were spread out in order not to present an easy target.

Sgt Garmory spotted a van that appeared to have several unusual slits in the rear doors. It was about 50 metres away when the sergeant raised his self-loading rifle to his shoulder. At that moment the entire patrol came under heavy machine gun fire from the van.

Sgt Garmory opened fire as the rapid automatic fire hit members of his patrol. After emptying his complete magazine into the back of the terrorists' wagon he gave a quick contact report and then, without any thought for his own life, changed his magazine and engaged the enemy again. Having realised that his men were seriously injured, Sgt Garmory then ran back,

Captain Robert Nairac of the Grenadier Guards who was murdered by the IRA in Northern Ireland. (MOD/Crown Copyright)

THE GUARDS 43

THE GRENADIER GUARDS

The Grenadiers were equipped with the Milan anti-tank missile in the 1980s. (DPL)

The tailor's shop where the Grenadiers' uniforms are prepared for ceremonial events. (MOD/Crown Copyright)

still under fire, picked up the light machine gun from a wounded Guardsman and fired that complete magazine at the still stationary van.

During that exchange of fire, the vehicle began to move away. Sgt Garmory then ran across the road, picked up the self-loading rifle of another wounded Guardsman and fired again at the vehicle as it drove off. Guardsmen Glen Ling, Kevin Johnson and Graham Duggan were killed in the attack. While it was not proven, evidence suggested that some of the terrorists were wounded or killed. The rear of the enemy vehicle was hit many times and enemy fire was halted at one stage as if to indicate that a man had been hit. Sgt Garmory was awarded the Military Medal, his commanding officer saying of him: "Sgt Garmory fought like a tiger. He showed a burning courage and a fighting spirit beyond praise. His actions were truly heroic."

Removing Saddam Hussein

Following the Iraqi invasion of Kuwait in 1991, the 1st Battalion Grenadier Guards was despatched along with its Warrior armoured infantry fighting vehicles from its base in

A Grenadier Guards Sergeant Major in the 1980s. (MOD/Crown Copyright)

Germany to join the Coalition forces being assembled to eject Saddam Hussein's forces. They then returned to London to troop their Colour on the Queen's Birthday Parade in 1992. Thereafter, they headed back to Northern Ireland for a six-month operational tour. In 1994, the 2nd Battalion Grenadier Guards was placed in suspended animation. Its traditions, dating all the way back to Lord Wentworth in the 17th century, are continued by the 2nd Battalion's Nijmegen Company, which today is based in London on public duties.

As the end of the decade approached, the Grenadiers found themselves facing a further period of intense activity. The 1st Battalion deployed to Bosnia on peace-keeping operations called Operation Grapple, wearing the United Nations blue berets and with its vehicles painted white. It provided security for supply convoys and maintained stability between the Croatian population and the Serbs. This initially included the UN peacekeeping missions in the former Yugoslavia known as the United Nations Protection Force (UNPROFOR). It later evolved into NATO's Implementation Force

Grenadier Guards boarding a Chinook helicopter during an exercise on Salisbury Plain in Wiltshire in 1991. (DPL)

(IFOR) and finally the Stabilisation Force in Bosnia and Herzegovina. (SFOR).

After the terror attack on the United States in 2001, the battalion was placed on high alert for security operations and was deployed around Heathrow Airport and Windsor in 2003 as a direct response to intelligence concerns of an imminent attack by al-Qaeda-linked militants armed with anti-aircraft missiles.

Service in The Balkans

A year later the Grenadiers were at high readiness as the spearhead lead battalion with the Queen's Company sent to Kosovo on internal security operations to restore order after rioting near Pristina. In 2004, the Grenadiers deployed to Bosnia on peace-keeping operations before returning to the UK to prepare for a tour in southern Iraq. The Grenadiers moved into Basra in May 2006 as part of 20 Armoured Brigade. During the following year, the battalion was sent to Afghanistan with 12 Mechanised Brigade with the task of training and mentoring the Afghan National Army and Police. The work ↪

In late 1992 the 1st Battalion deployed to Bosnia on peace-keeping operations called Operation Grapple, wearing the blue berets of the United Nations. (DPL)

THE GUARDS 45

THE GRENADIER GUARDS

Grenadiers in September 1999 during 'live fire' training in the Brecon Beacons in Wales. (DPL)

was challenging, and the Grenadiers found themselves operating in small teams to advise an entire Afghan Kandak (battalion). The Brigade's aim was to create stability and allow reconstruction to start by dominating the area as well as securing the main Sangin Valley.

Within a month of 12 Mechanised Brigade's arrival, the Taliban had launched its anticipated summer offensive. The insurgents increased their use of improvised explosive devices (IEDs) in an aggressive offensive. On May 3, 2007, the enemy mounted an attack on a checkpoint in Garmsir. ISAF reports indicated that as many as ten insurgents launched the attack with Rocket Propelled Grenades (RPGs) and small arms fire. At Patrol Base Delhi, Grenadier Guardsman Simon Davison, who was manning a General Purpose Machine Gun (GPMG), sustained a gunshot wound and was evacuated to Camp Bastion, but sadly later died.

In 2009 the battalion was back in southern Afghanistan, this time as the principal manoeuvre unit of 11th Light Brigade. The commander of Regional Command South, Major General Nick Carter, sent a clear message to the Taliban that the focus of operations over the next few months was to be in the ungoverned spaces in the district of Nad-e Ali, to the west and south west of Lashkar Gah. For General Carter and ISAF, securing Nad-e Ali and Marjah were an operational priority. In December, after three months of deliberations, President Obama announced that the United States would surge troop levels in Afghanistan to 30,000.

The regiment deployed numerous times to Afghanistan on a mission codenamed Operation Herrick. (MOD/Crown Copyright)

The Grenadiers deployed to Basra in southern Iraq in 2006 to take part in Operation Telic. (MOD/Crown Copyright)

Chinook helicopters flew LCpl Ashworth and his team to their objective in Afghanistan in 2012. As soon as they left the helicopter they came under heavy fire. (DPL)

THE GRENADIER GUARDS

When the aircraft landed, LCpl Ashworth and his team ran towards the enemy. (DPL)

LCpl Ashworth of the Grenadier Guards who was awarded the Victoria Cross. (MOD/Crown Copyright)

Key Roles and a New Threat

A major operation was planned in southern Afghanistan in which the Grenadiers would play a key role. However, a terrifying new threat was emerging. Afghan soldiers and policemen were turning their guns on British troops, under the influence of payment or intimidation by the Taliban. In November, a rogue Afghan policeman shot dead five soldiers: three from the Grenadier Guards and two from the Royal Military Police. All five had been mentoring the Afghan police in a compound where they had been working, living, and eating together. The Grenadiers were named as WO1 Darren Chant, Sgt Matthew Telford, and Guardsman James Major, along with Cpl Steven Boote and Cpl Nicholas Webster-Smith of the Royal Military Police.

On February 13, 2010, Operation Moshtarak commenced. The Grenadiers worked alongside the Coldstream and Scots Guards to help clear the Nad-e Ali area, which was home to hundreds of insurgents. In the preliminary mission to clear a route, Lance Sergeant David Greenhalgh, a

48 THE GUARDS

Communications in Helmand were a major priority as regiments deployed company groups to separate locations, known as Forward Operating Bases. (DPL)

member of the Queen's Company, 1st Battalion Grenadier Guards, was killed when his Jackal patrol vehicle struck an IED.

In 2012 the battalion deployed with 12 Mechanised Brigade on its third tour. Having arrived at Forward Operating Base Price (FOB Price) in the Nahr-e Saraj district, the Grenadiers held a small parade in the full heat of the Afghan sun on April 21, to mark the 70th anniversary of Her Majesty the Queen becoming their Colonel. The Queen had held the title of Colonel of the Regiment for ten years until her accession to the throne when she became the regiment's Colonel-in-Chief, a post she continued to hold with all five regiments of Foot Guards until her passing in 2022.

To mark the special occasion, the Queen's Company flag was flown over FOB Price. At the time Sergeant Richard Archer, 2 Section Commander, said: "To be in the Queen's Company is a fantastic privilege; there's intense rivalry between the companies, but this is the one everyone wants to be a part of due ↪

Before deploying to Helmand, the Grenadiers had been issued with grenade launchers that were fitted under the barrel of their SA80 assault rifles. (MOD/Crown Copyright)

THE GUARDS **49**

THE GRENADIER GUARDS

US President Donald Trump, escorted by the then HRH Prince of Wales, later King Charles III, inspects the Grenadier Guards in June 2019 during an official state visit. (MOD/Crown Copyright)

As well as helicopters Guardsmen deployed across Helmand in small, tracked Viking and Warthog vehicles. (DPL)

to the honour of having the Queen as our figurehead. I'd like to congratulate Her Majesty on this fantastic achievement and hopefully her association with the Queen's Company will continue for many years to come."

Bravery Under Fire
In June 2012, members of the Grenadiers' Reconnaissance Platoon, commanded by Captain Michael Dobbin, were inserted by helicopter to engage an insurgent sniper team that had previously ambushed a British patrol, killing three soldiers. The snipers had since been located in a compound by intelligence sources. The Guardsmen checked their equipment before boarding a Chinook helicopter to be flown out on to the ground. Among them was Lance Corporal James Ashworth, a dedicated young Guardsman who previously had served with the Guards Parachute Platoon, which forms 6 Platoon of B Company, 3rd battalion The Parachute Regiment. The Platoon came under fire almost as soon as it left the helicopter, prompting Lance Corporal Ashworth to lead his fire team in a charge over 300 metres to the heart of the enemy position in a nearby village. Two insurgents were killed in this initial assault.

As Ashworth was leading the charge, Captain Owen Davis, a Royal Marine officer attached to the Platoon, spotted an insurgent, believed to be a sniper, fleeing into a walled compound in the village. At that point, other Taliban insurgents entered the village to rescue their sniper team and engaged the Platoon from several positions. The immediate priority for Ashworth and his fire team was to flush the sniper from the compound in the village

The Grenadier Guards carried out pre-deployment training in early 2021 for a mission in Iraq. (MOD/Crown Copyright)

outbuilding. Accordingly, they split up, using grenades to clear all likely hiding places. Captain Davis was in the process of searching and clearing a corridor when the sniper emerged or, in Davis's words, 'popped out' and opened fire. "I returned fire," said Davis, "and hit him in the stomach and hip."

Despite his wounds, the sniper succeeded in taking cover in a room from which, despite being trapped, he continued to put up a fight and ignored calls for him to surrender. At that stage, the situation had reached a stalemate. The use of a rocket launcher or an air strike was ruled out because of the close proximity of the British personnel. LCpl Ashworth volunteered to break the stalemate by throwing his last grenade into the room, enabling Captain Dobbin and Captain Davis to carry out an assault as soon as it exploded. It was an act of heroism that cost LCpl Ashworth his life. ⊃

THE GRENADIER GUARDS

The Grenadier Guards with the Queen's casket at the gun carriage during Her Majesty's state funeral in 2022. (MOD/Crown Copyright)

The bearer party from the Grenadier Guards marches alongside the gun carriage carrying Her Majesty Queen Elizabeth II to her state funeral in 2022. (MOD/Crown Copyright)

Captain Michael Dobbin later said: "LCpl Ashworth was killed while fighting his way through compounds; leading his fire team from the front whilst trying to protect his men, and he showed extraordinary courage to close on a determined enemy. His professionalism under pressure and ability to remain calm in what was a chaotic situation is testament to his character."

For his action LCpl James Ashworth was awarded the Victoria Cross. He citation said: "His total disregard for his own safety in ensuring the last grenade was posted accurately was the gallant last action of a soldier who had willingly placed himself in the line of fire on numerous occasions earlier in the attack. This supremely courageous and inspiring action deserves the highest recognition."

The Modern Grenadiers

Since 2012, the Grenadiers have deployed to Brunei in 2014, Kenya in 2015 and 2016 and Belize in 2019. On operations the 1st Battalion formed the lead battlegroup for the NATO Very High Readiness Joint Task Force with Dutch, Estonian and Albanian companies under command.

In 2018 the battalion was directed to Iraq where it trained Iraqi and Kurdish forces in their fight against Islamic State. During the same tour, a company was seconded to Kabul as part of the Kabul Security Force, while another company was sent to South Sudan in support of the United Nations. During that time, the battalion sent companies to the Falkland Islands as part of the reinforcement mission and on counter-poaching operations in Africa. During that busy period the battalion trooped its Colour in 2015 and 2019 on the Queen's Birthday Parade.

Today, the Grenadiers serve as part of the Catterick-based 4th Light Brigade Combat Team in Yorkshire, assigned to the 1st (UK) Division. This is listed as an agile, lethal force ready for expeditionary operations. Created as a result of the government's Integrated Security and Defence Review, it will deliver a fully manned, modernised warfighting division by 2030. These capabilities will be built around a digitally networked combination of the new Ajax reconnaissance platform, the new Boxer armoured personnel carrier, the upgraded Challenger 3 main battle tank and the Apache AH64E battlefield attack helicopter, as well as long-range precision fires and un-crewed aerial systems.

Future operations for the Grenadier Guards are being re-modelled around Brigade Combat Teams (BCTs), creating more self-sufficient tactical formations, and providing more options for decision makers. BCTs integrate the full range of capabilities but at the lowest possible level, including artillery, un-crewed aerial systems, cyber, air defence, engineers, signals, and logistical support.

The Grenadier Guards is being shaped into an army that will increase its ability to deliver effect in the deep physical and virtual battlespace. New capabilities which the Grenadiers will see in the next five years will include disposable drones, cyber and electromagnetic capability to enhance infantry activity and chest-worn electronic maps that are fully integrated with a rear headquarters.

In March 2023, the King decorated all eight Grenadier Guardsmen who carried Her Majesty's coffin at her funeral in 2022. (MOD/Crown Copyright)

THE GUARDS 53

SUBSCRIBE
TO YOUR FAVOURITE MAGAZINE
AND SAVE

Britain at War is dedicated to exploring every aspect of Britain's involvement in conflicts from the turn of the 20th century through to modern day. From World War I to the Falklands, World War II to Iraq, readers are able to re-live decisive moments in Britain's history through fascinating insight combined with rare and previously unseen photography.

shop.keypublishing.com/bawsubs

GREAT SUBSCRIPTION OFFERS FROM

FlyPast is internationally regarded as the magazine for aviation history and heritage. Having pioneered coverage of this fascinating world of 'living history' since 1980, *FlyPast* still leads the field today. Subjects regularly profiled include British and American aircraft type histories, as well as those of squadrons and units from World War One to the Cold War.

shop.keypublishing.com/fpsubs

Aeroplane traces its lineage back to the weekly The Aeroplane launched in June 1911, and is still continuing to provide the best aviation coverage around. *Aeroplane* magazine is dedicated to offering the most in-depth and entertaining read on all historical aircraft.

shop.keypublishing.com/amsubs

Order direct or subscribe at:
shop.keypublishing.com

Or call **UK 01780 480404** Overseas **+44 1780 480404**
Lines open 9.00-5.30, Monday-Friday

A Coldstream Guards Drill Sgt ensures his Guardsmen are standing in straight lines. (MOD/Crown Copyright)

THE COLDSTREAM GUARDS

'Nulli Secundus' – Second To None

The Coldstream Guards is the oldest continuously serving regular regiment in the British Army. Although founded earlier than the First Regiment of Foot Guards, the Grenadiers, the regiment was placed second to them in the order of precedence, as the Grenadiers had spent longer in the service of the Crown. However, when on parade with the other regiments of Foot Guards, the Coldstream Guards takes its position on the left of the line thus standing, as their motto says, Nulli Secundus - Second To None.

THE COLDSTREAM GUARDS

Today, the regiment has one battalion which serves as a light role infantry unit rotating between operational readiness and public duties, the latter usually performed by Number 7 Company, based in London. Tourists can easily spot the Coldstream Guards when they are on parade by the red plume worn on the right side of their bearskins, their tunic buttons that sit in pairs and the garter star worn on their shoulders.

The bearskin that the Guardsmen proudly wear is 18in tall and weighs several pounds. The original idea behind this large headdress was to make soldiers appear bigger so as to intimidate their enemy when standing face-to-face in line on the battlefield. Today, the bearskin in only worn on parade. It must be groomed, washed and the curb chain polished. The bearskins are made from the Canadian black bear; under Canadian law no more than 5% of the wild bear population, estimated to be around 600,000, can be culled annually. Of the 'legally harvested' black bear pelts, the UK Ministry of Defence buys fewer than 100 every year for use in producing new bearskins.

Prior to the state funeral of Her Majesty Queen Elizabeth II, the Coldstream Guards was among the units that supported the continuous vigil at Her Majesty's lying-in-state in Westminster Hall. Each period of 24 hours was divided into four watches. Except for the first and last, each of the 20 watches lasted for six hours. Within each watch, a vigil lasted for 20 minutes.

The regiment also played an important role in the funeral procession, providing a guard of honour outside Buckingham Palace consisting of 101 Guardsmen. They stood steadfast, the only indicator for them that the funeral procession was nearing was the 'five-minute bike' – a police outrider who preceded the main procession to alert the troops lining the route that the procession would be approaching shortly. The lone outrider had a yellow diamond fixed to the front of his bike for easy recognition.

The Coldstream Guards was first formed in 1650 at Berwick, Northumberland, during the English Civil War by Colonel George Monck, who had begun his career as a Royalist but had later joined Cromwell after the defeat of the King. The Guards was therefore part of the English Parliamentarian forces and was known as 'Monck's Regiment of Foot'. It was soon in action at the Battle of Dunbar in the same year. Thereafter, Monck marched his regiment across into England at the village of Coldstream before heading south on a five-week march to London where he eventually supported the restoration of the monarchy in 1660. The town of Coldstream, situated on the River Tweed near Berwick-upon-Tweed, would later be adopted as the name of the regiment and would become one of its recruiting regions.

Monck was awarded the Order of the Garter for his support of King Charles II and the regiment was assigned to keep order in London.

Subsequently, the King decided to retain the regiment for his personal security in addition to the bodyguard formed during his exile in 1656 as the 1st Regiment of Foot Guards, which became the Grenadier Guards.

The Rebirth of Monck's Regiment

In 1661 Monck's Regiment symbolically laid down its arms as part of the New Model Army but was immediately ordered to take them up again as the 'The Lord General's Regiment of Foot Guards' in service of the King. After

The Coldstream Guards at Trooping the Colour, an annual event at which each of the Foot Guards marks the monarch's birthday. (MOD/Crown Copyright)

Monck's death, the Earl of Craven took command, and the regiment adopted the new name of the Coldstream Regiment of Foot Guards.

The Coldstreamers went on to serve during the Monmouth Rebellion in 1685, when the 1st Duke of Monmouth (the King's nephew) unsuccessfully attempted to overthrow the unpopular King James II, fighting at the decisive Battle of Sedgemoor in Somerset. The Coldstream Guards thereafter took part in the Nine Years War against the French, in the battles of Walcourt and Landen and the Siege of Namur in the Spanish Netherlands. During the War of Spanish Succession, six companies of Coldstream Guards participated in various operations along the Spanish and Portuguese coasts. They reinforced the garrison during the Siege of Gibraltar in 1704, then formed part of the force that captured Barcelona in May 1708. Perhaps the Coldstream's' finest hour was at the defence of Hougoumont, a fortified chateau complex south of Brussels in Belgium, positioned in front of the right-hand side of the Allied line during the Battle of Waterloo in 1815. It was there that the Coldstream

The Coldstream Guards, red plumes in their bearskins, at the Queen's Birthday Parade. (MOD/Crown Copyright)

Guards famously closed the huge gates at the entrance to the complex, trapping a small French detachment inside the courtyard and stopping further assaults by them. The French then stormed the gate which the battalion, supported by men of the Scots Guards, shut again. The action at Hougoumont was a vital strategic success on the battlefield; it was attacked throughout the day by thousands of French infantry but the Coldstream Guards held out to the end.

The Coldstream Guards served in the Crimean War where four members of the regiment, Private William Stanlake, Brevet-Major John Augustus Conolly, Brevet-Major Gerald Littlehales Goodlake, and Private George Strong were each awarded the Victoria Cross for their extreme valour. A 'Brevet' rank indicates that the individual has been promoted in the field, often after an act of bravery. Private Strong from Yeovil in Somerset removed a live shell from his trench which would have killed many of his colleagues. He had already received the Crimea Medal with Sevastopol clasp, as well as the Turkish Crimea Medal. He was

The Coldstream Guards famously closed the huge gates at the entrance to Hougoumont Chateau, south of Brussels in Belgium, in 1815. (MOD/Crown Copyright)

THE GUARDS 59

THE COLDSTREAM GUARDS

Coldstream Guardsmen fighting in Crimea in the 1880s went into battle wearing bearskin caps and tunics. (MOD/Crown Copyright)

personally decorated by Queen Victoria on June 26, 1857. His medals sold at auction for £71 in 1907 and were purchased by Lieutenant E G Christie-Miller, an officer in the Coldstream Guards, who presented them to the regiment.

In 1914, the Coldstream Guards consisted of four battalions with the 1st at Aldershot, the 2nd and the 4th (Pioneer) at Windsor and the 3rd at Chelsea Barracks. A fifth reserve battalion was raised in 1915. In August 1914, following the outbreak of World War One, all three regular battalions of the Coldstream Guards were landed at Le Havre and advanced to the Belgian frontier. These units soon found themselves on the retreat from Mons, covering some 200 miles in just 13 days. The 4th Battalion was also deployed, while the 5th was held in the UK and sent soldiers forward to replace those injured and killed. Private Thomas Whitham, aged 29, was initially posted to the 5th Battalion before being sent to join the 1st Battalion in France to take part in the brutal fighting at Ypres in Belgium. In July 1917, his company of Coldstream Guards was pinned down by machine gun fire. Private Whitham, on his own initiative, immediately worked his way from shell hole to shell hole up to the German position and although under very heavy fire, captured it together with an enemy officer and

Coldstream Guards of the 4th Battalion take a break in the fighting at the battle of Passchendaele in 1917. (MOD/Crown Copyright)

60 THE GUARDS

A light tank in 1943. These vehicles were used by the Coldstream Guards in Europe. (MOD/Crown Copyright)

Vehicles of the Guards' armoured division in the North African desert in early 1943. (MOD/Crown Copyright)

two other ranks. This bold action was of great assistance to the battalion and undoubtedly saved many lives. For his selfless courage Whitham was awarded the Victoria Cross. After the war he became a bricklayer but struggled to find work and was forced to pawn his VC and other medals. Unemployed and homeless, he died at Oldham Royal Infirmary near Manchester on October 24,1924, aged just 34.

Life at the Front
The Coldstream Guards fought on the Western Front in what became a campaign of grinding attrition, with each side trying to blast each other into submission. Soldiers lived in terrible conditions, fighting in mud and constantly in fear of gas attacks. Rations were basic, but they did receive packets of tea and biscuits. The biscuits were produced under government contract by Huntley and Palmers, which in 1914 was the world's largest biscuit manufacturer. The biscuits were notoriously hard and had to be soaked in tea or water to be enjoyed.

At the outbreak of World War Two in 1939, the 1st and 2nd Battalions of the Coldstream Guards deployed to Europe with the British Expeditionary Force (BEF) and in 1940 were evacuated from Dunkirk in France. The 1st Battalion was converted to an armoured unit ➲

THE GUARDS 61

THE COLDSTREAM GUARDS

The Coldstream Guards conduct a 'parade rehearsal' in working dress on Horse Guards. (MOD/Crown Copyright)

in 1941 and a year later it received Crusader tanks in readiness for a role with the Guards Armoured Division. It remained at home until June 1944, when it took part in the Normandy campaign, joined by the 4th and 5th Battalions. In France, the regiment participated in the battles for Caen and Falaise. It then fought its way across northwest Europe with some elements of the 1st Battalion taking part in the ground force that linked up with the 1st Airborne Division at Arnhem in September 1944. It ended the war at Lubeck on the German Baltic coast in May 1945.

In late 1942, the 2nd Battalion deployed to Tunisia in North Africa with the 1st Guards Brigade, remaining there until March 1944 before moving to the Italian campaign. At the outbreak of war the 3rd Battalion was serving in Egypt. It joined the North Africa campaign but was captured at Tobruk in Libya in June 1942. It was reformed later that year and remained in the desert war until early 1943, when it deployed to Syria. In March 1944 the battalion transferred to the Italian front where it faced fierce fighting and heavy losses.

In 1943, near the port of Salerno in Italy, thousands of Allied soldiers waged a fierce campaign against German forces. One of the bloodiest encounters was on the now infamous Hill 270. The Grenadier Guards had already been engaging in a ferocious battle with German Panzer-Grenadiers and had been rebuffed. On September 25, 1943, the 3rd Battalion Coldstream Guards was sent forward with the intention of launching an attack at midday. It was hoped that this would be an audacious assault, using a line of trees near the base of the hill as cover. It would be followed by a two-company assault on the hilltop position.

As the attack went in, German forces offered strong resistance. The Coldstream Guards suffered heavy casualties under a barrage of German small arms fire and mortar shells. Many of the battalion's officers were killed as German machine gun teams held the high ground. Company Sergeant Major (CSM) Peter Wright took charge and single-handedly silenced three Spandau machine gun teams with grenades and his bayonet. He then led his men to consolidate the position and move forward. Having re-grouped, he organised and led an assault to defeat a German counterattack. For his outstanding courage, he was awarded the Distinguished Conduct Medal but King George VI cancelled the award and replaced it with the VC when he was made aware of the full extent of CSM Wright's actions.

The 3rd Battalion captured Hill 270, but at great cost. During the battle Lance Corporal Ronald Blackham was killed, aged 21. His body was lost for decades until it was rediscovered by a team of Italian historians using metal detectors. They also discovered the bodies of two other Coldstream Guardsmen. Only one of the three bodies, Lance Corporal Blackham, was identified, his regiment being confirmed by the buttons and cap badge that had once adorned his uniform. On March 16, 2017,

The Coldstream Guards maintains its ceremonial role when not deployed on operations. (MOD/Crown Copyright)

In 2004 the Scot Guards deployed to Basra as part of the 4th Armoured Brigade and used the enhanced protection of Warriors APVs. (DPL)

Jungle warfare training is conducted by all Foot Guards regiments. (MOD/Crown Copyright)

Ballymurphy area. It was accommodated in former police stations and a converted factory where temporary rooms were built. The soldiers often slept in bunk beds and used sleeping bags. The Scots Guards found itself facing riots and ongoing attacks throughout its tour in the Province and facing accusations of prejudice from Catholics on the grounds that it was a Protestant regiment.

Early in 1972 the 2nd Battalion, saved from suspended animation by the deteriorating security situation in Northern Ireland, moved to Germany, but was shortly afterwards despatched to the Province where it was based in Armagh through 1973. In the following year the IRA conducted an attack in mainland Britain, murdering 18-year-old Guardsman William Forsyth and his colleague John Hunter, just 17. Both were killed by a bomb planted by the IRA at the Horse and Groom pub in Guildford, Surrey, not far from their base at the Guards depot. In 1975, the 2nd Battalion was once again back in Northern

THE GUARDS 83

THE SCOTS GUARDS

The Warthog armour-protected vehicle was used to ferry troops across Helmand. (DPL)

Ireland and operating in the Divis Flats area of Belfast. More tours followed in the late 1970s, 80s and 90s.

Once More to Northern Ireland

In May 1990, the 2nd Battalion was again deployed to South Armagh, operating across Cullyhanna, north of Crossmaglen – a town in the south of the county that had a notorious reputation for IRA attacks. The terrorists saw the area as their heartland and attempted to intimidate the Army by placing signs in the region warning of 'sniper operations'. Lance Sergeant Graham Stewart from Perth, serving with the 2nd Battalion, was on foot patrol in Cullyhanna when he and his fellow Guardsmen passed a derelict house from which a gunman launched a machine gun attack. He was flown to hospital in Belfast but sadly died from his wounds. He was just 25 years old. The Scots Guards' last deployment to Northern Ireland came in 2001.

After the Argentines invaded the Falklands on April 2, 1982, an initial Task Force was despatched by sea three days later on 5 April. It was then quickly identified that, in addition to the Royal Marines and two Parachute Regiment battalions heading south with 3 Commando Brigade RM, a second brigade should be at readiness to move. Accordingly, 5th Infantry Brigade, including the Welsh Guards, 7th Duke of Edinburgh's Own Gurkha Rifles and the 2nd Battalion the Scots Guards, was put on notice to move. On May 12 they sailed for the South Atlantic, many of the personnel aboard the cruise liner *Queen Elizabeth 2*, which had been converted for military operations at short notice in Southampton.

On the morning of June 13, 1982 the Scots Guards force was moved by helicopter from its position at Bluff Cove to an assembly area near Goat Ridge, west of Mount Tumbledown, in preparation for a night attack. From there it would advance to a start-line in readiness for the assault. A small force of Scots Guards mounted a diversionary attack south of Mount Tumbledown, supported by the Scimitars of the Blues and Royals.

G Company was tasked with securing the western end of the mountain as the assault commenced. Then Left Flank (a company) would pass through the area taken by G Company to capture the centre of the summit. Finally, Right Flank would pass through Left Flank's position and secure the eastern end of Tumbledown. In his orders group with his company commanders beforehand, the commanding officer had concluded that the long uphill assault across the harsh ground of Tumbledown would be suicidal in daylight.

In Helmand, the Scots Guards took part in Operation Moshtarak to clear insurgents from key area of Helmand. It was the biggest British helicopter-borne assault since the Gulf War in 1991. (MOD/Crown Copyright)

Accordingly, to help identify the bunkers in the night assault, Guardsmen fired flares at the summit and used 66mm shoulder-fired light anti-tank weapons (LAW) and 84mm medium anti-tank weapons to clear enemy positions. However, the Argentinians remained firm and refused to budge.

Meanwhile, two Royal Navy frigates, HMS *Yarmouth* and HMS *Active*, were bringing down salvos of naval gunfire support on the enemy, prior to the Scots Guards fighting its way slowly up the mountain. The Guardsmen were often pinned down by machine gun and sniper fire in what was recounted later as a 'bloody exhausting fight'. With bayonets fixed the soldiers finally captured the feature after experiencing some of the most savage hand-to-hand fighting of the conflict. Nine members of the battalion were killed and 43 wounded.

Liberating Kuwait

Eight years later, in late 1990, the Scots Guards was assigned to the UK's contribution to the Coalition force that was destined for Kuwait after Iraqi forces invaded the Gulf state in August 1990 and refused to withdraw. UK ground forces arrived in Kuwait as divisional troops with the 1st Armoured Division and began training for Operation Granby, the mission to eject Saddam Hussein's forces from Kuwait.

In 1993 the 2nd Battalion deployed to Canada to take part in a six-week exercise at the British Army Training Unit Suffield (BATUS).

The Scots Guards served across Helmand and was in the vanguard of the mission to re-take Musa Qaleh. (MOD/Crown Copyright)

On its return, however, the battalion at last fell prey to defence cuts and was placed in suspended animation. In 1998, the 1st Battalion moved to Ballykinler in Northern Ireland on a two-year residential tour.

In 2004 the 1st Battalion deployed to Basra in southern Iraq during Operation Telic as part of 4th Armoured Brigade, reinforcing security in the city on a six-month tour. The Scots Guards patrolled on foot and in mobile patrols in support of the Iraqi police. Two years later, in 2006, the battalion commenced the 'Bowman radio conversion' programme as the Army's new communication system came into service. This culminated in an armoured infantry exercise in Poland during which temperatures sank to -27°C. This was followed by an intense package of pre-deployment training for simultaneous

THE SCOTS GUARDS

Operating in support of the Afghan National Army was a priority as the mission in the country came to an end. (DPL)

deployments to Afghanistan and Iraq. Right Flank company was bound for Helmand and the remainder of the battalion to Basra. In 2007 the battalion returned for a second tour as part of 4th Mechanised Brigade, minus Right Flank that had been deployed to Helmand. In Iraq, the Scots Guards faced tragedy in December 2007 when Guardsman Stephen Ferguson, 31, from Lanarkshire, was killed when his Warrior armoured infantry fighting vehicle slid into a canal in Basra.

On November 1, 2007, British forces started preliminary operations in preparation for the assault to re-take Musa Qaleh in northern Helmand. The mission began on December 7, with US airstrikes hitting Taliban targets. The 1st Battalion Scots Guards and elements of 40 Commando RM formed a blocking position to the south of the town.

In early 2010 the Scots Guards were back in Helmand as one of the fighting units assigned to Operation Moshtarak. Its aim was to drive the Taliban from its stronghold areas in central Helmand around Marjah and Nad-e Ali and then hold and reinforce that success. The operation would see three of the Foot Guards regiments operating alongside each other – the Scots Guards' Right Flank, the 1st Battalion Coldstream Guards and the 1st Battalion Grenadier Guards. They were specifically tasked with mounting an air assault into the northern Nad-e Ali district, known as the 'heart of darkness'. It was the biggest British helicopter-borne assault since the Gulf War in 1991 and Operation Moshtarak was itself the biggest joint operation since the 2001 invasion of Afghanistan. As the operation got underway, on February 18, 2010, LSgt David 'Davey' Walker of 1st Battalion Scots Guards was fatally wounded when his patrol came under heavy Taliban fire while conducting a routine framework patrol. He was serving with the Right Flank of the Scots Guards, attached to Combined Force Nad-e Ali (North).

In April 2010, the 1st Battalion Scots Guards was back in Helmand as part of 4th Mechanised Brigade. The battalion had only been on the ground for a few days when Colour Sergeant Alan Cameron was seriously injured by an improvised explosive device while on foot patrol north of Lashkar Gah on April 13. He was flown back to the UK but succumbed to his wounds and died in March of the following year.

Two months later, on July 10, 2010, LCpl Stephen Daniel Monkhouse was killed. He had been operating in a Joint patrol with the Royal

A sniper provides cover for soldiers advancing forward during an operation in southern Afghanistan. (MOD/Crown Copyright)

86 THE GUARDS

The Scots Guards at Her Majesty Queen Elizabeth's state funeral in 2022. Those members of the regiment who carried the coffin in Edinburgh were decorated by the King in March 2023 for their service. (MOD/Crown Copyright)

Dragoon Guards (RDG) providing security during the construction of a road called Route Trident, north of Lashkar Gah. Their team came under insurgent fire that killed LCpl Monkhouse and Cpl Matt Stenton of the RDG. On August 1, 2010, LSgt Dale Alanzo McCallum was shot dead during an operation near Lashkar Gah when his checkpoint came under fire.

Working with the Afghan Police
In late 2012, the 1st Battalion the Scots Guards returned to southern Afghanistan for its last tour, deploying once again with 4th Mechanised Brigade. Guardsmen from Headquarter Company were based at Forward Operating Base Ouellette, working alongside the Afghan National Police to bring security and allow freedom of movement for traffic on Route 611, as the drawdown of UK forces increased, and command and control was passed to the Afghan National Army.

Camp Bastion was built in early 2006 in readiness for the arrival of the first battle group in the same year. It was the operational hub of British and coalition forces throughout the campaign. At the height of the Helmand mission the UK had 137 bases across Helmand, all of which were either handed over to the Afghan National Security Forces in 2014 or closed. Members of the Scots Guards were among the last troops to leave Helmand after handing over their base to Afghan forces in 2013. At the time Lieutenant Colonel Robert Howieson, commanding officer of the 1st Battalion The Scots Guards, said: "The Afghans are now capable of delivering their own security in this area and therefore it is the right time to redeploy our troops home." A special album, called *From Helmand to Horse Guards*, was produced by the pipes and drums of the 1st Battalion The Scots Guards and was released in 2022 as a tribute to comrades who had died in Helmand. At the time of the album's release in June 2011, the battalion was in London to troop its Colour on The Queen's Birthday Parade.

And in May 2023, elements of the Scots Guards as well as the Household Division headed the ceremonial parade in London for the coronation of King Charles III. The parade included 6,000 members of the armed forces with the Household Cavalry and the five regiments of Foot Guards taking centre stage.

THE GUARDS 87

THE IRISH GUARDS

THE IRISH

'Quis Separabit' – Who Shall Separate Us

Members of **the Irish Guards** are universally known as 'The Micks'. They dress the buttons on their tunics in sets of four to signify their position in the Foot Guards. They wear a shamrock emblem on their tunic collars and a St Patrick's Star on their shoulder epaulettes, and they can also be easily identified by the St Patrick's blue plume worn on the right side of their bearskins. In addition to their ceremonial excellence, the main role of the 1st Battalion Irish Guards is to deliver dismounted infantry for close combat, most recently in Iraq and Afghanistan.

Guardsmen of the regiment with shamrock in their caps at a parade to mark St Patrick's Day. (DPL)

GUARDS

The regiment was officially formed by order of Queen Victoria on April 1, 1900, to mark the bravery and courage of the Irish regiments during the Boer War. Irishmen serving in other regiments of the Guards were encouraged to transfer to the new regiment. This included the first Regimental Sergeant Major who was serving with the Scots Guards but transferred to the Irish Guards with great alacrity. In 1902, the Irish Wolfhound Club presented a puppy to the regiment as a mascot and it was named Brian Boru after the 11th century Irish king. The tradition of the Irish Guards having a wolfhound mascot remains to this day. On St Patrick's Day 1901, boxes of shamrock were sent to the regiment by Queen Alexandra, wife of Edward VII.

The Regimental Colour of the Irish Guards carried during the Trooping the Colour parade. (MOD/Crown Copyright)

The wolfhound mascot of the Irish Guards, who parades at all ceremonial events with the regiment. (MOD/Crown Copyright)

THE GUARDS

THE IRISH GUARDS

1st Battalion, Irish Guards prepare to leave Wellington Barracks in London following the outbreak of World War One. The battalion arrived in France as part of the British Expeditionary Force on August 13, 1914. (MOD/Crown Copyright)

The tradition of this Royal gift is repeated every year in a special parade.

As part of a re-organisation of the British Army in 2020, the Irish Guards became part of the 11th Security Force Assistance (SAF) Brigade, specialist in delivering training to build the military capabilities of our allies and partners. Most notably it took the lead in training the armed forces of Ukraine as part of a wider programme of support to the country in its defence against Russian aggression. As part of this training the Irish Guards has overseen a programme of military training to Ukrainian forces focussed on tactics called 'fighting in built-up areas' (FIBUA) as well as the use of anti-tank N-LAW missiles and unmanned aerial platforms. The restructure delivered an additional benefit to the Irish Guards with the reactivation of Number 9 and 12 Companies that had been lost when the 2nd Battalion was placed into suspended animation in 1947. Both companies will be based in London as Foot Guards Public Duties Companies, whilst resurrecting the traditions and ethos of the 2nd Battalion.

In December 2022, following the passing of Her Majesty Queen Elizabeth II, the King approved a series of new military appointments. HRH Prince

Guardsmen of the 1st Battalion Irish Guards, advancing north of Anzio in Italy during January 1944. (MOD/Crown Copyright)

In late 1915 the British introduced the hand grenade 'Number 1' – featuring a stick that had a long handle. It was issued to the Irish Guards in 1916 but in the confinement of the trenches the long handle became a liability. (MOD/Crown Copyright)

HRH the Princess of Wales visits the Irish Guards on Salisbury Plain in 2023 in her new role as Colonel of the Regiment. (MOD/Crown Copyright)

William, as the new Prince of Wales, was appointed Colonel of the Welsh Guards while HRH the Princess of Wales was appointed as Colonel of the Irish Guards. Her Royal Highness has a long association with the Irish Guards and has presented the shamrock to them on St Patrick's Day for several years.

Shortly after her appointment, Her Royal Highness visited the 1st Battalion on Salisbury Plain in Wiltshire where it participated in training Ukrainian soldiers. She was shown how the regiment operates and took part in a demonstration of combat medical training. Lance Corporal Jodie Newell, 25, who was in charge of instructing the Princess, said: "I was so nervous. I'm teaching the Princess of Wales med [medicine] – it was an honour. We were just showing her what we medics do in the Army. She was actually really good, really eager to take part." The Princess was also briefed about anti-vehicle and anti-personnel mine clearance and was shown the weapons systems used by the Irish Guards. As part of the visit, she met Guardsmen of No 1 and No 2 Companies, who told her about their recent experiences in training park rangers in East Africa in methods to counteract poaching.

Keeping up Morale

After World War One was declared on August 4, 1914, hundreds of volunteers and reservists packed the boat trains from Ireland to Liverpool as they headed for London to join the Irish Guards – the public mood confident that by Christmas the war would be all over. The humour, discipline and daring of these young men helped create a regiment with a special character, always able to laugh in the face of adversity while delivering gallant heroism on the battlefield.

In 1914, the 1st Battalion quickly embarked for France within a week of hostilities being declared, and thereafter remained on the Western Front for most of the war. It took part in the Battle of Mons, which was considered a strategic victory for Germany. The British stand at Mons slowed but did not stop the advance of the enemy into France. In the retreat from Mons on September 1, the Commanding Officer of the 1st Battalion, Lieutenant Colonel The Honourable George Morris, was killed in action. The fighting was intense and by then thoughts that the war would end by December had faded. The Irish Guards faced some of the bloodiest fighting of 1914 at the First Battle of Ypres. The original 1st Battalion, which had arrived in France barely two months earlier, had been practically wiped out in the intense German assault and had to be reconstructed with new recruits from the 2nd and 3rd Battalions.

As well as the enemy, the Guardsmen fought the winter weather conditions. Appropriate clothing was limited and conditions in the trenches were freezing. Driving rain and bitter temperatures left soldiers suffering a range of cold injuries and no matter how hard they ➲

The Irish Guards and units across the British Army deployed in the Arabian Peninsula in 1967 were based in a tented camp in the mountains of Radfan, an area north of Aden on the border with Yemen. (DPL)

THE GUARDS 91

THE IRISH GUARDS

The pipe band of the Irish Guards. (MOD/Crown Copyright)

tried to keep their weapons clean, everything was often covered in mud. With many troops falling ill due to the cold, the War Department issued woollen jumpers and goatskin coats. Duckboards were introduced in the trenches – which for many soldiers indicated that they were going to be in the muddy conditions for some time. Rudyard Kipling's son John, often called Jack, had been commissioned into the Irish Guards at just 17 years of age. He was sent to France in August with the 2nd Battalion. Sadly, Lieutenant John Kipling was later reported missing in action in September 1915 during the Battle of Loos.

In January, the Irish Guards was ordered to prepare for an attack on German positions near the town of Cuinchy in northern France in response to a German advance. The town straddled La Bassée Canal and the enemy seized an area known as the 'Hollow'. This was strategically important as it defended a culvert under a railway embankment. A company of Irish Guards was ordered to join the Coldstream Guards and retake the position, but they met with heavy fire that left many of them dead or wounded. A second assault stalled under fire until LCpl Michael O'Leary, who was an orderly to a young officer, charged forward, killing five Germans manning a machine gun that was sited on high ground. He advanced and attacked a second position, covering almost 60 yards towards the second machine gun. The enemy didn't see O'Leary before he opened fire, killing three Germans, and taking two prisoners. For his actions that day he received a battlefield promotion to sergeant on February 4 and was subsequently awarded the Victoria Cross. His citation stated: "O'Leary practically captured the enemy's position by himself and prevented the attacking party from being fired upon." He was presented with his VC by King George V in a private ceremony at Buckingham Palace on June 22, 1915. George Bernard Shaw later wrote a play inspired by his story called *O'Flaherty VC* and his actions were used to promote recruitment in the regiment.

HRH Prince Edward presents shamrock on St Patrick's Day in the early 1990s. (DPL)

The Irish Guards was not initially deployed to Northern Ireland but in 1992 the regiment was sent to Fermanagh where it often operated from helicopters. (DPL)

A New Weapon

In late 1915 the British introduced the hand grenade 'Number 1', featuring a stick that had a long handle. It was issued to the Irish Guards in 1916 but in the confined spaces of the trenches the long handle became a liability. When Guardsmen reached back to throw the grenade, the fuse could strike the trench wall behind them and ignite. The Belgian Army had developed a self-igniting hand grenade and the War Department in London pressed the munitions factory William Mills to develop a similar grenade. The result was the first British hand grenade ever to be issued on a large scale and it became known as the 'Mills Bomb'. Resembling a small pineapple, it was officially called the Mills Number 5 and its segmented casing was designed to fragment – although soldiers said it rarely did.

Throughout 1916 and 1917, the Irish Guards fought bravely on the blood-soaked battlefields of the Somme and Passchendaele despite suffering severe casualties. It participated in the Third Battle of Ypres and the Battle of Cambrai before conducting attacks on the Hindenburg line in the final days of the war. A week after, it took part in the Victory Parade in London to celebrate the end of the war and the 2nd Battalion was placed in suspended animation. Few could have predicted that 20 years later, in 1939, it would be reformed for another conflict.

The years in between the wars saw the Irish Guards recover and consolidate at its base in Aldershot, Hampshire. At the Guards Depot in Caterham, Surrey, No 5 Company Irish Guards joined a staff that included a company from each regiment of Foot Guards tasked with turning recruits into smart young guardsmen. ➲

Irish Guards celebrate St Patrick's Day while deployed in the Balkans in 1999. (DPL)

THE GUARDS 93

THE IRISH GUARDS

At the outbreak of World War Two, in September 1939, rumours were rife as to where the Irish Guards would first be deployed. The 1st Battalion was sent to reinforce Norway while the 2nd Battalion helped cover the evacuation of the Dutch royal family from the Hook of Holland before being tasked to reinforce Boulogne as the British Expeditionary (BEF) force prepared to evacuate from Dunkirk. Thereafter, the 1st Battalion, as part of 24th Guards Brigade, took part in the North African campaign and it was at Djebel Bou Azoukaz in Tunisia where the Irish Guards faced stiff opposition from the enemy.

Bravery Recognised

In one encounter on April 28, 1943, the battalion faced an imminent attack from a large formation of Germans. LCpl John Kenneally charged on his own initiative down a forward slope and rushed the enemy, firing his Bren gun from the hip. He ran straight at them and caught them by surprise. The shock and

Irish Guards dismount from a Warrior during their deployment in Kosovo in 1999. (DPL)

An Irish Guardsman during the intervention into Kosovo. (DPL)

The Irish Guards was among the first units into Basra in the south of Iraq in 2003. (MOD/Crown Copyright)

awe of his attack forced the enemy to scatter. Two days later he repeated his daring action when he spotted the enemy forming up to attack. Accompanied by a sergeant, Kenneally charged the Germans again, he and his fellow Micks firing their weapons as they advanced. Kenneally was badly wounded but refused to give up. His courage won him the Victoria Cross and two years later Winston Churchill, in a post-war speech given in May 1945, mentioned his bravery. The post-war years would see Kenneally promoted to sergeant and joining the newly formed 1st Guards Parachute Battalion.

The 1st Battalion Irish Guards subsequently moved to the Italian front and took part in the Anzio landings in 1944. Meanwhile, the 2nd and 3rd Battalions went to serve in France with the Guards Armoured Division, taking part in the Normandy campaign in June 1944. Thereafter, in September 1944, they led the vanguard of 30 Corps in the thrust north through Belgium and Holland

The Irish Guards remained ready for ceremonial events throughout their busy period of operations from Kosovo to Iraq and Afghanistan. (MOD/Crown Copyright)

A line of Warrior armoured personnel vehicles of the Irish Guards heading towards Kosovo from Macedonia during the NATO intervention in 1999. (MOD/Crown Copyright)

Gwartheg, gwartheg ym mhob man – rhowch lonydd iddynt!

Yn India, mae'r fuwch yn cael ei gwarchod a'i charu. Mae'n cael crwydro o gwmpas, ac mae bob amser yn cael ei thrin yn dyner ac yn garedig – a gyda diolchgarwch mawr.

Mae nifer o bethau da yn deillio o'r fuwch, pethau sy'n gwella bywydau pobl. Felly mae'n bwysig eu gwarchod a'u cadw.

Dywedodd Gandhi, a fu unwaith yn arweinydd ar India: 'Gwarchod gwartheg ydy rhodd Hindŵaeth i'r byd.'

> Gwnewch restr o'r holl gynhyrchion sy'n dod o'r fuwch. Meddyliwch am ffyrdd y gall pobl ddangos eu bod yn ddiolchgar am gynnyrch y ddaear yn ein gwlad ni. Efallai y bydd eich athro'n rhoi taflen waith i chi i'ch helpu.

> Gyda phartner, neu mewn grwpiau bach, gwnewch *collage* neu beintiwch lun sy'n dangos y pethau da y mae pobl yn eu cael o'r byd ar un ochr – a sut y dylent ofalu am y byd a bod yn ddiolchgar ar yr ochr arall.

Felly byd pwy ydy hwn?

Trwy gydol y llyfr hwn, rydych chi wedi darganfod rhai pethau pwysig iawn am ateb y cwestiwn hwn:

- Mae yna lawer o bethau sydd wedi'u distrywio yn y byd
- Mae'n fyd hyfryd, yn llawn lliw a phrydferthwch
- Bodau dynol sydd wedi achosi peth o'r distryw yma
- Mae yna bethau da a phethau drwg yn y byd
- Mae gan fodau dynol gyfrifoldeb arbennig yn hyn o beth
- Mae creadwyr crefyddol o'r farn bod dyletswydd arnom ni i ofalu am fyd Duw
- mae rhai pobl yn ceisio clirio'r llanast

A phan ystyriwch chi hyn yn ofalus, fe welwch chi mai rhodd arbennig iawn yw'n byd ni, un y mae'n rhaid gofalu amdano.

A'r rheswm am hyn ydy mai ni sy'n gyfrifol - er mai byd Duw ydy hwn !

Geirfa a mynegai

adnoddau	tud.7	arian neu ddeunyddiau y gellir eu defnyddio
alergedd	tud.11	pan y mae'ch corff yn ymateb yn gryf i rywbeth e.e. paill neu lwch
cymuned	tud.7	pobl sy'n byw yn yr un ardal, neu grŵp sydd â rhywbeth yn gyffredin rhyngddynt
dharma	tud.10, 21	gair yr Hindŵ am ddyletswydd; rhywbeth y dylech ei wneud
llygru	tud.3	baeddu rhywbeth, yn enwedig trwy ychwanegu rhywbeth niweidiol
mudiad	tud.22	elusen neu grŵp sy'n gweithio gyda'i gilydd
sanctaidd	tud.14	cysegredig, ar wahân – ar gyfer Duw neu er mwyn cyflawni rôl bwysig iawn
stiward	tud.10, 18	rhywun sy'n gofalu am rywbeth ar ran rhywun arall